Collins

Cambridge Lower Secondary

Maths

PROGRESS BOOK 7:
STUDENT'S BOOK

Author: Alastair Duncombe

William Collins' dream of knowledge for all began with the publication of his first book in 1819.
A self-educated mill worker, he not only enriched millions of lives, but also founded a flourishing publishing house.
Today, staying true to this spirit, Collins books are packed with inspiration, innovation and practical expertise.
They place you at the centre of a world of possibility and give you exactly what you need to explore it.

Collins. Freedom to teach.

Published by Collins

An imprint of HarperCollinsPublishers
The News Building, 1 London Bridge Street, London, SE1 9GF, UK

HarperCollinsPublishers
Macken House, 39/40 Mayor Street Upper, Dublin 1, D01 C9W8, Ireland

Browse the complete Collins catalogue at
collins.co.uk

British Library Cataloguing-in-Publication Data
A catalogue record for this publication is available from the British Library.

The questions and accompanying marks included in this resource have been written by the author and are for guidance only.
They do not replicate examination papers and the questions in this resource will not appear in your exams. In examinations
the way marks are awarded may be different. Any references to assessment and/or assessment preparation are the author's
interpretation of the syllabus requirements.

This text has not been through the endorsement process for the Cambridge Pathway. Any references or materials related
to answers, grades, papers or examinations are based on the opinion of the author. The Cambridge International Education
syllabus or curriculum framework associated assessment guidance material and specimen papers should always be referred to
for definitive guidance.

Author: Alastair Duncombe
Publisher: Elaine Higgleton
Product manager: Catherine Martin
Product developer: Saaleh Patel
Copyeditor: Eric Pradel
Proofreader: Tim Jackson
Cover designer: Gordon MacGilp
Cover illustrator: Ann Paganuzzi
Typesetter: Ken Vail Graphic Design
Production controller: Sarah Hovell
Printed in India by Multivista Global Pvt. Ltd.

Content

Introduction

This *Stage 7 Progress Student's Book* supports the *Collins Cambridge Stage 7 Lower Secondary Maths course*.

The book contains
- six Assessment Tasks – each corresponding to 4 or 5 chapters in the Collins Cambridge Stage 7 Maths course
- two End of Book Tests: Paper 1 is a non-calculator paper and Paper 2 is a calculator-allowed paper
- Self-assessment sheets for each of the Assessment Tasks and End of Book Tests.

How to use the Progress resources

This Student's Book contains a range of Assessment Tasks and Tests that are designed to assess your learning. They can be used to identify your strengths and weaknesses. The resources can also be used by your teachers to guide their teaching to make sure you make the best possible progress through the course.

The six Assessment Tasks could be used as class tests or your teachers may ask you to complete them at home. Each Task includes a list of the topics being tested, and begins with some multiple choice questions. These starting questions are designed to help build confidence and to check your understanding of some key ideas. As you work through each task, you will find the questions become more challenging. You will find that some questions are designed to be answered without a calculator, whilst a calculator is allowed in other questions.

Some of the questions in each Task are written to address the Cambridge *Thinking and Working Mathematically* characteristics:
- Specialising and generalising
- Conjecturing and convincing
- Characterising and classifying
- Critiquing and improving.

These questions may require you to think more deeply. You may also need to explain your answer or show clear working out.

The End of Book tests contain questions assessing the topics you will have covered in the whole year. The style of the End of Book tests is the same as the Assessment Tasks, with a mixture of question styles and question difficulties, as well as the inclusion of some Thinking and Working Mathematically questions. Your teachers may use these tests to assess your progress during the year.

The Self-assessment sheets give you the opportunity to reflect on your understanding. You record the mark for each question in the grids and then use these to find how well you have done with the questions relating to each chapter (or, for the End of Book Tests, each mathematics strand). This allows you to then reflect on which parts of the test went well and which areas you found harder. You could pick out particular chapters as strengths or weaknesses. You could also comment on your success with *Thinking and Working Mathematically* questions or how you did on calculator or non-calculator questions.

The Self-assessment sheets also prompt you to set some targets. Try not to set targets that are too general. You are more likely to achieve your targets if you write something more specific. For example,

Less helpful targets...

To become more confident at decimals ✗

To avoid making needless errors ✗

More helpful targets...

To become more confident at dividing a decimal by a whole number ✓

To try to avoid making needless errors by underlining key words in the question ✓

Key features: Assessment Tasks

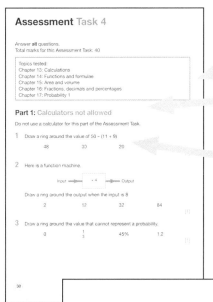

At the top of each Assessment Task, you will find a list of the topics being covered.

You will be told whether you can use a calculator or not.

Each Task begins with some multiple-choice questions to boost your confidence and to assess key ideas.

Each Task contains some questions that relate to Thinking and Working Mathematically. You may have to think more deeply in these questions.

Each question is worded clearly and there is plenty of space for you to show your working out.

Key features: Student self-assessment sheets

Assessment Task 1: Self-assessment

Enter the mark for each question in the unshaded cells below.

Question	Negative numbers, indices and roots	2D and 3D shapes	Collecting data	Factors and rational numbers
1				
2				
3				
4				
5				
6				
7				
8				
9				
10				
11				
12				
13				
14				
15				
16				
17				
18				
19				
20				
Total	/10	/9	/4	/7

> Record the mark you scored in each question in the table.

> Add up the marks in each column. The totals will help you to compare how you have done in each topic area.

Some of the questions test your skills at Thinking and Working Mathematically. Write your marks for these questions in the grid below.

Question number	6	7	8	14	16(b)	17	18	20	Total
Thinking and working mathematically									/13

The areas of the test that I am pleased with are

_____

_____

_____

The areas of the test that I found harder are

_____

_____

_____

> There is space for you to reflect on how you have done and to set some targets.

Set yourself TWO targets.

TARGET 1

_____

TARGET 2

_____

Assessment Task 1

Answer **all** questions.
Total marks for this Assessment Task: 30
You will need mathematical instruments.

Do **not** use a calculator for this Assessment Task.

Topics tested:
Chapter 1: Factors
Chapter 2: 2D and 3D shapes
Chapter 3: Collecting data
Chapter 4: Negative numbers and indices

1   Draw a ring around the number that is a multiple of 9

102   142   168   261

[1]

2 The diagram shows a circle with centre O.

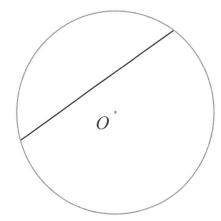

Draw a ring around the name given to the line that has been drawn inside the circle.

circumference   chord   diameter   radius

[1]

3 Draw a ring around the value of $\sqrt{64}$

4   8   16   32

[1]

4 Mario wants to find out what nurses working in his hospital think about how much they are paid.

He selects 30 nurses from his hospital at random.

Draw a ring around the population in Mario's study.

All nurses that work in his hospital   All people that work in his hospital

The 30 nurses he selects   All nurses in the country

[1]

5 A 3D shape has 1 curved surface and 2 circular faces.

Draw a ring around a type of shape that it could be.

sphere   pyramid   cylinder   cone

[1]

6 Draw a ring around an example of continuous data.

the colour of a bus   the number of passengers on the bus

the length of a bus   the type of fuel used by the bus

[1]

7 Work out:

8 ÷ (−2)   _____

[1]

8 Complete the following working to find the lowest common multiple of 12 and 15.

First 6 multiples of 12 are: 12, 24, _____, _____, _____, _____

First 6 multiples of 15 are: 15, 30, _____, _____, _____, _____

The lowest common multiple of 12 and 15 is _____

[2]

9 Sanjay is investigating what members of his gym think about the equipment.

(a) He decides to collect data using one of these two methods.

Method 1	**Method 2**
Ask every member of his gym what they think.	Ask a sample of gym members what they think.

Give a reason why he may prefer to use Method 2.

_____

_____

[1]

(b) The gym has 500 members.
Sanjay suggests collecting data from 10 members.

Tick (✓) a box below to show if Sanjay's sample size is appropriate or not.

Appropriate sample size ☐   Not an appropriate sample size ☐

Give a reason for your answer.

_____

_____

[1]

10 The diagram shows two congruent triangles.

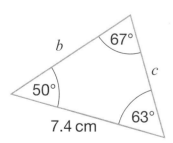 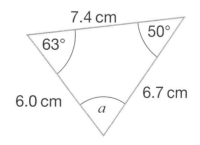

Not to scale

Tick (✓) to show if each statement is true or false.

	True	**False**
Angle $a = 67°$	☐	☐
Side length $b = 6.0$ cm	☐	☐
Side length $c = 6.7$ cm	☐	☐

[1]

11 Here is a list of integers.

$$2 \quad -2 \quad -3 \quad 4 \quad -4 \quad -7 \quad 8 \quad 14$$

Use four of these integers to complete these calculations.
Use each integer no more than once.

_____ × _____ = −28

_____ × _____ = −28

[1]

12 Here is a circle and a radius OA.

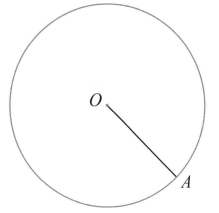

Not to scale

(a) Line L passes through A and is perpendicular to OA.

Draw line L on the circle.

[1]

(b) Write down the mathematical name for line L.

_____

[1]

13 Draw lines to match each calculation with its answer.

−12 − 26   −38

−12 − (−26)   −14

26 − (−12)   14

−7 − 7   38

[1]

14 Here are three prisms.

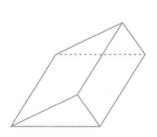

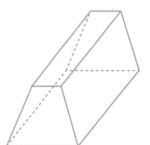

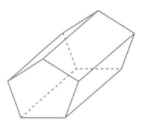

_____ edges   _____ edges   _____ edges

Find the number of edges for each prism and then complete the statement.

The number of edges of a prism must always be a multiple of _____

[2]

15 Find the value of $\sqrt[3]{125} - 5^2$

_____

[2]

16 Find a number between 5010 and 5020 that is a multiple of 8

_____

[1]

17 Samira designs a questionnaire to find out information about how frequently people go to the supermarket.

Here is one of her questions and the tick boxes.

Question → | How many times do you go to the supermarket?
Tick (✓) a box.

Tick boxes → 1 to 2 ☐   3 to 4 ☐   4 or more ☐

(a) Explain how Samira could improve her question.

_____

_____

[1]

(b) Explain what is wrong with Samira's tick boxes.

_____

_____

[1]

18 ■ represents a square number.

◆ represents a cube number.

■ + ◆ = 63

Find the value of ■ − ◆

_____

[2]

19 Ellie has 48 yellow counters and 72 red counters.

She wants to divide these counters into pots such that:

- she uses all her counters
- each pot contains exactly the same number of yellow counters
- each pot contains exactly the same number of red counters.

(a) Find the largest number of pots Ellie can use.

_____

[2]

(b) Find the total number of counters that would be in each pot.

_____

[1]

20 Here is a rule for testing if a number is divisible by 7.

> Remove the last digit from the number and double it.
>
> Subtract this from the remaining number.
>
> If the answer is divisible by 7, then so was the original number.

Use this rule to show that 672 is divisible by 7.

[2]

Total marks: $\dfrac{}{30}$

7

Assessment Task 1: Self-assessment

Enter the mark for each question in the unshaded cells below.

Question	Factors	2D and 3D shapes	Collecting data	Negative numbers and indices
1				
2				
3				
4				
5				
6				
7				
8				
9				
10				
11				
12				
13				
14				
15				
16				
17				
18				
19				
20				
Total	/9	/7	/6	/8

Some of the questions test your skills at Thinking and Working Mathematically. Write your marks for these questions in the grid below.

Question number	9(a)	9(b)	13	14	16	17(a)	17(b)	20	Total
Thinking and working mathematically									/10

The areas of the test that I am pleased with are

_____

_____

_____

The areas of the test that I found harder are

_____

_____

_____

Set yourself TWO targets.

TARGET 1

_____

_____

TARGET 2

_____

_____

Assessment Task 2

Answer **all** questions.
Total marks for this Assessment Task: 30
You will need mathematical instruments.
You may find tracing paper helpful.

Do **not** use a calculator for this Assessment Task.

Topics tested:
Chapter 5: Expressions
Chapter 6: Symmetry
Chapter 7: Rounding and decimals
Chapter 8: Presenting and interpreting data 1

1   Here is an expression: $2x + y + 3$

Draw a ring around the number of terms in this expression.

1	2	3	4

[1]

2   Draw a ring around the number of lines of symmetry in a regular octagon.

1	2	4	8

[1]

3   Draw a ring around the value that is the same as 2×10^2

20	40	200	400

[1]

4   A bag contains b books.
Anushka removes 2 books from the bag.

Draw a ring around the expression for the number of books now in the bag.

$b + 2$	$b - 2$	$2b$	$\dfrac{b}{2}$

[1]

5 Draw a ring around the value of −0.4 + 0.9

    0.5   −0.5   −1.3   1.3

[1]

6 Lauren sells jumpers.

The Venn diagram shows some information about the number of red jumpers and the number of large jumpers she sold last week.

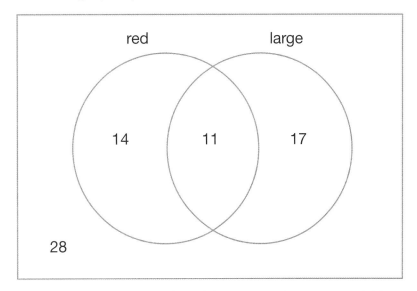

Draw a ring around the number of red jumpers Lauren sold last week.

    11   14   25   28

[1]

7 Here are four decimals.

    0.516   0.5137   0.5145   0.51542

Write each decimal in the correct position in the table.

Rounds to 0.51 (to 2 decimal places)	Rounds to 0.52 (to 2 decimal places)

[2]

8 Find the value of $3c$, when $c = 6$

....

[1]

9 Calculate 0.4×116

....

[2]

10 The two-way table shows some information about the favourite subjects for students in Class A and students in Class B.

	Science	Maths	Art	History	Other
Class A	7	4	6	5	
Class B	6	8	8	2	5

(a) There are 30 students in Class A.

Complete the table.

[1]

(b) Find the total number of students in the two classes that gave Science or Maths as their favourite subject.

....

[1]

11 Find the value of $318 \div 10^4$

....

[1]

12 Here are the values of a and b.

$a = 6$ $b = 2$

Complete each statement by writing an expression involving **both** a and b.
One has been done for you.

$2a + b$ .... $= 14$

.... $= 10$

.... $= 3$

[2]

13 (a) Here are two shapes.

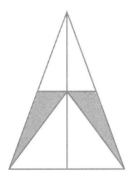   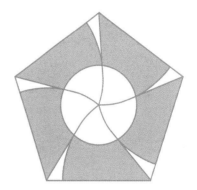

Order ....   Order ....

Write down the order of rotational symmetry for each shape.

[2]

(b) Here is a square divided into 16 smaller squares, with two of them shaded.

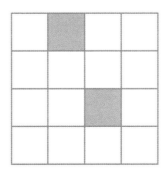

Shade exactly **six** more small squares to give a design with rotational
symmetry of order 2 and no lines of symmetry.

[2]

14 Pari, Mel and Kieron each think of a number.

Pari's number is a.
Mel's number is b.
Kieron's number is c.

They each do some calculations on their number.

Complete the table by writing in the missing expressions and numbers.
The first one has been done for you.

	Expression
Pari multiplies her number by 2	$2a$
Mel multiplies her number by 5 and then subtracts 2	
Kieron multiplies his number by _____ and then adds _____	$4c + 9$

[2]

15 Maxine grows two types of potato plant in her garden.

The table shows how many small potatoes and how many large potatoes her plants produced this year.

	Small	Large
Type A	15	9
Type B	23	11

Draw a compound bar chart to represent this information.
Remember to complete the key.

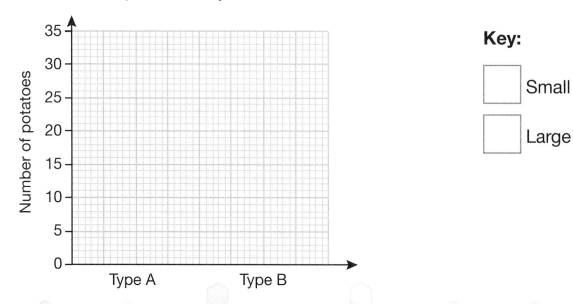

Key:

☐ Small

☐ Large

[2]

16 Calculate $21.34 \div 9$

Give your answer to 3 decimal places.

_____

[2]

17 The values of x, y and z are:

$x = 8$, $y = 6$ and $z = 5$

Find the value of $xy - 3z$

_____

[2]

18 The frequency diagram shows the hand span (in centimetres) of a group of students.

Show that over half of the students have a hand span of less than 18.5 cm.

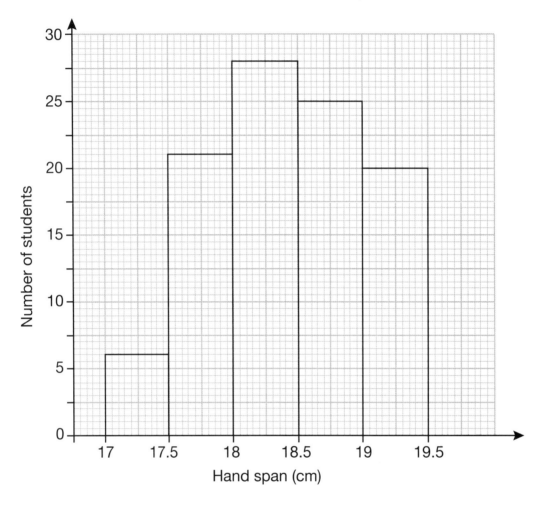

[2]

Total marks: $\dfrac{}{30}$

Assessment Task 2: Self-assessment

Enter the mark for each question in the unshaded cells below.

Question	Expressions	Symmetry	Rounding and decimals	Presenting and interpreting data 1
1				
2				
3				
4				
5				
6				
7				
8				
9				
10				
11				
12				
13				
14				
15				
16				
17				
18				
Total	/9	/5	/9	/7

Some of the questions test your skills at Thinking and Working Mathematically. Write your marks for these questions in the grid below.

Question number	7	12	13(b)	18	Total
Thinking and working mathematically					/8

The areas of the test that I am pleased with are

_____

_____

_____

The areas of the test that I found harder are

_____

_____

_____

Set yourself TWO targets.

TARGET 1

_____

_____

TARGET 2

_____

_____

Assessment Task 3

Answer **all** questions.
Total marks for this Assessment Task: 30

Topics tested:
Chapter 9: Fractions
Chapter 10: Manipulating expressions
Chapter 11: Angles
Chapter 12: Measures of average and spread

Part 1: Calculators not allowed

Do not use a calculator for this part of the Assessment Task.

1 Draw a ring around the answer to $1\frac{2}{7} + 1\frac{3}{7}$

$2\frac{5}{7}$ $1\frac{5}{7}$ $2\frac{5}{14}$ $1\frac{5}{14}$

[1]

2 Draw a ring around the size of angle a.

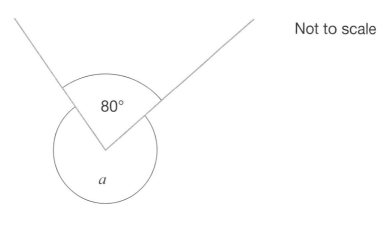

Not to scale

100° 120° 220° 280°

[1]

3 Draw a ring around the fraction that is the value of $\frac{2}{7} \times \frac{1}{3}$

$\frac{3}{21}$ $\frac{2}{21}$ $\frac{3}{10}$ $\frac{2}{10}$

[1]

4 The table shows the marks that a group of students obtained in a test.

Marks	Number of students
5	11
6	8
7	6
8	3
9	2

(a) Write down the modal mark.

_____

[1]

(b) Find the range of the marks.

_____

[1]

5 Tick (✓) to show if the answer to each calculation is less than 1 or greater than 1.

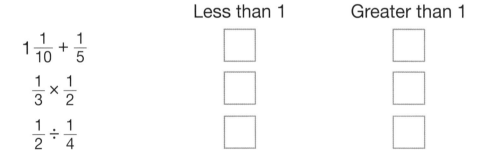

	Less than 1	Greater than 1
$1\frac{1}{10} + \frac{1}{5}$	☐	☐
$\frac{1}{3} \times \frac{1}{2}$	☐	☐
$\frac{1}{2} \div \frac{1}{4}$	☐	☐

[1]

6 Simplify.

$m \times m \times m =$ _____

[1]

7 Calculate.

$$\frac{2}{3} \div \frac{5}{12}$$

Give your answer in its simplest form.

_____

[2]

8 The diagram shows a parallelogram.

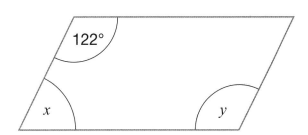

Not to scale

Calculate the size of angles x and y.

$x =$ _____ °

$y =$ _____ °

[2]

9 A bucket contains $2\frac{5}{6}$ litres of water.

Mia adds $1\frac{7}{10}$ litres of water to the bucket.

Show that the bucket now contains $4\frac{8}{15}$ litres of water.

[2]

10 Simplify.

$$\frac{n}{3} + \frac{4n}{9}$$

[2]

Part 2: Calculators allowed

You may use a calculator for this part of the Assessment Task.

11 Simplify $6h \times 2$

Draw a ring around your answer.

$8h$ $\qquad$ $12h$ $\qquad$ $6h^2$ $\qquad$ $36h^2$

[1]

12 The diagram shows two parallel lines, an angle marked t and four shaded angles.

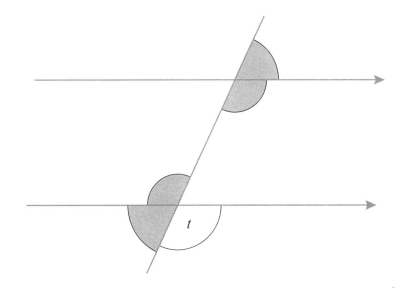

How many of the shaded angles are equal in size to angle t?

Draw a ring around your answer.

1 $\qquad$ 2 $\qquad$ 3 $\qquad$ 4

[1]

13 Draw a ring around the expression equivalent to $2(k + 3)$

$k^2 + 6$ $\qquad$ $k^2 + 5$ $\qquad$ $2k + 5$ $\qquad$ $2k + 6$

[1]

14 Dev records the number of glasses of water 15 people drink one day.

3	1	2	2	5	0	1	0
4	6	0	1	2	4	3	

Find the median number of glasses of water.

_____

[2]

15 The lines ABC and BD are perpendicular.

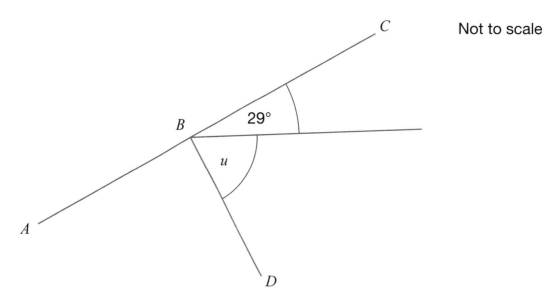

Not to scale

Find the size of angle u.

$u = $ _____ °

[1]

16 The table shows the number of trees in each of 50 gardens.

Number of trees	Number of gardens
0	9
1	18
2	12
3	6
4	5

(a) Calculate the mean number of trees in a garden.

_____

[2]

(b) Another garden has 10 trees.

Tina calculates the mean, median, mode and range for the number of trees in the 51 gardens.

She compares these values with the values for the original 50 gardens.

Some of the values are different and some of the values are the same.

Tick (✓) to show which values are different and which are the same.

	Different	The same
Mean	☐	☐
Median	☐	☐
Mode	☐	☐
Range	☐	☐

[2]

25

17 The diagram shows two parallel lines and a transversal.

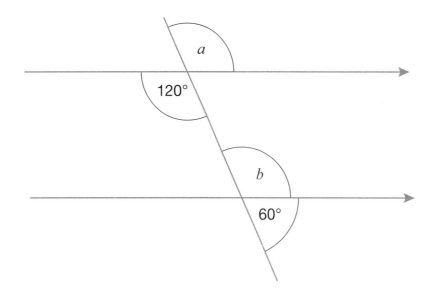

Not to scale

Write down the size of angles a and b.

$a =$ _____ °

$b =$ _____ °

[1]

18 Simplify each expression.

$4(3x - 2) + 8$

_____

$11 - 5a - 2 + 3a$

_____

[2]

19 Calculate the size of angle x.

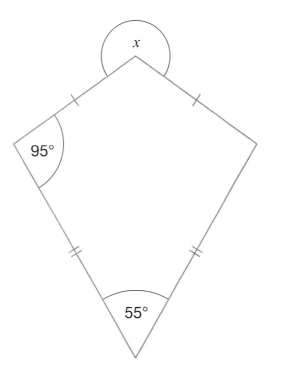

Not to scale

$x =$ _____ °

[2]

Total marks: $\dfrac{}{30}$

Assessment Task 3: Self-assessment

Enter the marks for each question in the unshaded cells below.

Question	Fractions	Manipulating expressions	Angles	Measures of average and spread
1				
2				
3				
4				
5				
6				
7				
8				
9				
10				
11				
12				
13				
14				
15				
16				
17				
18				
19				
Total	/7	/7	/8	/8

Some of the questions test your skills at Thinking and Working Mathematically. Write your marks for these questions in the grid below.

Question number	5	9	12	16(b)	Total
Thinking and working mathematically					/6

The areas of the test that I am pleased with are

_____

_____

_____

The areas of the test that I found harder are

_____

_____

_____

Set yourself TWO targets.

TARGET 1

_____

_____

TARGET 2

_____

_____

Assessment Task 4

Answer **all** questions.
Total marks for this Assessment Task: 40

Topics tested:
Chapter 13: Calculations
Chapter 14: Functions and formulae
Chapter 15: Area and volume
Chapter 16: Fractions, decimals and percentages
Chapter 17: Probability 1

Part 1: Calculators not allowed

Do not use a calculator for this part of the Assessment Task.

1   Draw a ring around the value of 50 – (11 + 9)

       48   30   20   –30

                                                                            [1]

2   Here is a function machine.

Input ➡ ×4 ➡ Output

Draw a ring around the output when the input is 8

       2   12   32   84

                                                                            [1]

3   Draw a ring around the value that cannot represent a probability.

       0                $\frac{1}{3}$ 45%   1.2

                                                                            [1]

4 Complete the table to show equivalent fractions, decimals and percentages.

Fraction	Decimal	Percentage
	0.75	
$\dfrac{3}{10}$		
		9%

[2]

5 Calculate.

(a) 0.35 + 0.8 + 0.65 + 2.2

_____

[1]

(b) $\dfrac{2}{3} \times 11 \times 3$

_____

[1]

6 Write a number on the answer line to make a correct statement.

1 hectare < _____ m² < 2 hectares

[1]

7 Write a number in each gap to make correct statements.

$(7^2 + 2 \times 3) \div 5 =$ _____

$(11 -$ _____ $) \times (9 + 3) = 36$

[2]

8 **(a)** Show that $\frac{5}{6} > \frac{37}{48}$

[1]

(b) Here are four fractions.

$\frac{19}{48}$ $\qquad$ $\frac{1}{3}$ $\qquad$ $\frac{11}{24}$ $\qquad$ $\frac{5}{12}$

Complete each sentence by writing one of the four fractions.

The smallest fraction is _____

The largest fraction is _____

[1]

9 There are 5 vowels (A, E, I, O and U) in the English language alphabet.

Tariq has 10 cards.

Liz gives Tariq two more cards with a letter on each.

The letters on these cards are not shown.

Tariq says, "If I now pick up one of my 12 cards at random, the probability it is a vowel is 0.25"

Write a letter on the two cards above to make Tariq's statement true.

[1]

10 The diagram shows a shape made from joining a rectangle and a right-angled triangle.

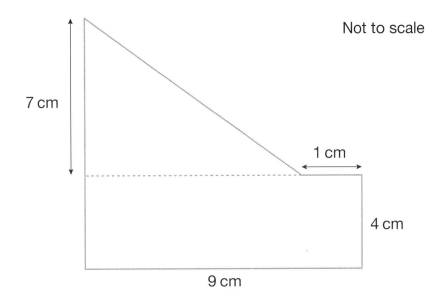

Not to scale

7 cm

1 cm

4 cm

9 cm

The total area of the shape is x cm².

Show that x is a square number.

[3]

11 Add a set of brackets in this calculation to make it correct.

$7 + 4^2 + 5 \times 2 = 49$

[1]

12 Here is a decimal number:

1.035

(a) Write 1.035 as a percentage.

_____%

[1]

(b) Write 1.035 as an improper fraction.

Give your answer in its simplest form.

_____

[2]

Part 2: Calculators allowed

You may use a calculator for this part of the Assessment Task.

13 An ordinary, fair six-sided dice is thrown.

Draw a ring around the probability of throwing a 4.

$\dfrac{1}{6}$ $\qquad\qquad$ $\dfrac{1}{4}$ $\qquad\qquad$ $\dfrac{4}{6}$ $\qquad\qquad$ $\dfrac{1}{2}$

[1]

14 The diagram shows a triangle.

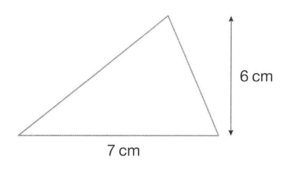

Not to scale

6 cm

7 cm

Draw a ring around the area of the triangle.

10.5 cm² $\qquad$ 13 cm² $\qquad$ 21 cm² $\qquad$ 42 cm²

[1]

15 Draw a ring around the formula for the number, h, of hours in d days.

$h = \dfrac{d}{24}$ $\qquad$ $h = 24d$ $\qquad$ $h = 2 + 24$ $\qquad$ $h = d - 24$

[1]

16 Insert one of the symbols

$$= \quad \textbf{or} \quad \neq$$

to compare each fraction and decimal.

The first one has been done for you.

$\dfrac{1}{6}$ _____ $\neq$ _____ 0.2

$\dfrac{11}{20}$ _____ 0.55

$\dfrac{7}{8}$ _____ 0.875

$\dfrac{5}{16}$ _____ 0.315

[2]

17 Here are three words:

COOKBOOK REAPPEAR WELLNESS

A letter is picked at random from each word.

Complete the table by listing the possible outcomes for each word and tick (✓) to show if the outcomes are equally likely or not.

The first row is completed for you.

Word	List of possible outcomes	Outcomes equally likely	Outcomes not equally likely
COOKBOOK	C, O, K, B		✓
REAPPEAR	_____		
WELLNESS	_____		

[2]

18 A bag contains 8 balls.

(1) (2) (3) (4) (5) (6) (7) (8)

Without looking in the bag, Martina picks a ball at random.

Tick (✓) to show if each of these statements is true or false.

Statement	True	False
It is probable that Martina will pick a number greater than 2.	☐	☐
It is possible that Martina will pick a number that is a factor of 9.	☐	☐
It is equally likely that Martina will pick a square number as it is that she picks an odd number.	☐	☐

[1]

19 (a) Here is an inequality for a decimal number x.

$1.49 < x < 1.5$

Write down a possible value for x.

_____

[1]

(b) Here is an inequality for a mixed number y.

$2\frac{1}{10} < y < 2\frac{1}{5}$

Write down a possible value for y.

_____

[1]

20 Write these areas in order of size, starting with the smallest.

0.04 m²   5 cm²   700 mm²

_____   _____   _____

smallest   →   →   largest

[1]

21 The diagram shows a cuboid.

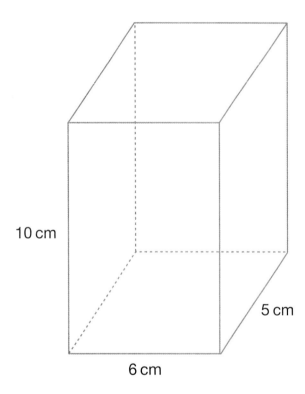

Not to scale

10 cm

5 cm

6 cm

Calculate the total surface area of the cuboid.

_____ cm²

[3]

22 Here are two function machines.

Function machine A

$x \longrightarrow \boxed{+6} \longrightarrow 20$

Function machine B

$x \longrightarrow \boxed{\times 5} \longrightarrow ?$

When x is the input to function machine A, the output is 20.

Find the output when the same value of x is the input to function machine B.

....

[2]

23 Biscuits are packed into packets.

The number of biscuits, b, in p packets is given by the formula $b = 6p$

The packets of biscuits are packed into boxes.
10 packets of biscuits are packed into each box.

Find a formula for the number of biscuits, b, in n boxes.

$b =$ ....

[1]

24 Here are two cuboids.

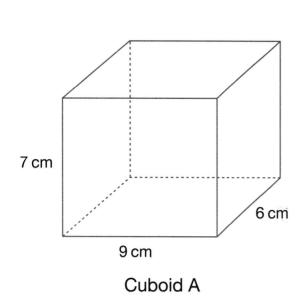 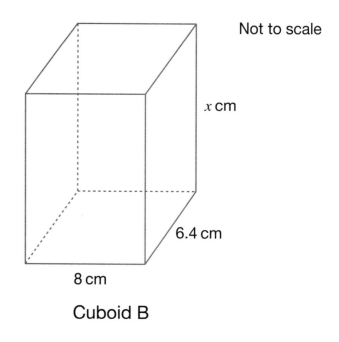

Not to scale

7 cm

6 cm

9 cm

Cuboid A

x cm

6.4 cm

8 cm

Cuboid B

| volume of cuboid B = volume of cuboid A + 6 cm³ |

Find the value of x.

$x =$ _____

[3]

Total marks: $\dfrac{}{40}$

40

Assessment Task 4: Self-assessment

Enter the marks for each question in the unshaded cells below.

Question	Calculations	Functions and formulae	Area and volume	Fractions, decimals and percentages	Probability 1
1					
2					
3					
4					
5					
6					
7					
8					
9					
10					
11					
12					
13					
14					
15					
16					
17					
18					
19					
20					
21					
22					
23					
24					
Total	/6	/5	/12	/11	/6

Some of the questions test your skills at Thinking and Working Mathematically. Write your marks for these questions in the grid below.

Question number	6	8(a)	9	10	18	19(a)	19(b)	Total
Thinking and working mathematically								/9

The areas of the test that I am pleased with are

_____

_____

_____

The areas of the test that I found harder are

_____

_____

_____

Set yourself TWO targets.

TARGET 1

_____

_____

TARGET 2

_____

_____

Assessment Task 5

Answer **all** questions.
Total marks for this Assessment Task: 40
You will need mathematical instruments.
Tracing paper may be used.

> Topics tested:
> Chapter 18: Transformations
> Chapter 19: Percentages
> Chapter 20: Presenting and interpreting data 2
> Chapter 21: Equations and inequalities
> Chapter 22: Ratio and proportion

Part 1: Calculators not allowed

Do not use a calculator for this part of the Assessment Task.

1   The point A has coordinates (5, 9).

Point A is translated 2 units right and 3 units down.

Draw a ring around the coordinates of the image of A.

   (7, 12)   (7, 6)   (3, 12)   (3, 6)

[1]

2   Here is an equation.

   $3x = 12$

Draw a ring around the value of x.

   $x = 3$ $x = 4$ $x = 9$ $x = 36$

[1]

3   A bus ticket increases by 25%

What is the new cost of the ticket as a percentage of the original cost?
Draw a ring around your answer.

   1.25%   25%   75%   125%

[1]

4 A school football team plays five matches.

The line graph shows the number of parents watching each match.

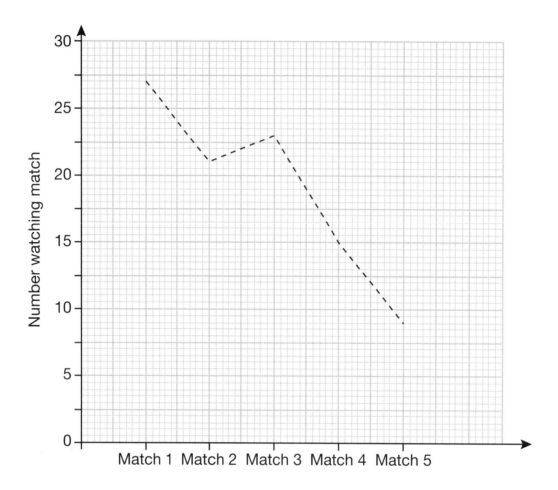

Find how many more parents watched Match 1 than watched Match 5.

_____

[2]

5 Find 0.5% of 800

_____

[1]

6 Here are five statements about ratios.

Draw lines to show whether each statement is true or false.
The first one has been done for you.

| Statement A |
| 12 : 15 = 4 : 5 |

| Statement B |
| 18 : 24 = 3 : 4 |

| Statement C |
| 4 : 6 = 3 : 5 |

| Statement D |
| 1.5 : 3 = 1 : 2 |

| Statement E |
| 0.6 : 0.4 = 2 : 3 |

| True |

| False |

[2]

7 **(a)** Show the inequality $x < 7$ on the number line.

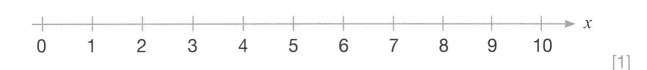

[1]

(b) Write an inequality to describe the interval shown on the number line.

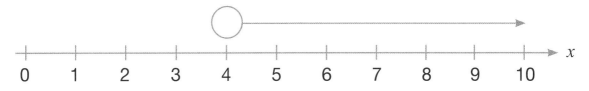

_____

[1]

8 **(a)** Rotate triangle T about the centre O by 180°

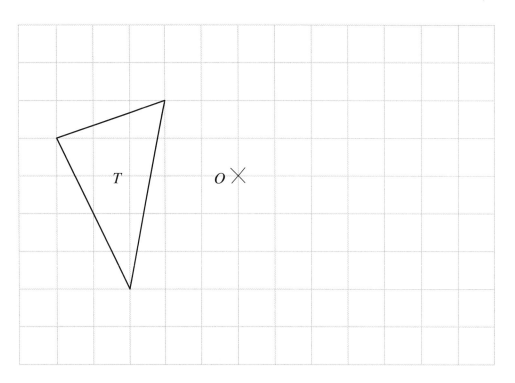

[1]

(b) Rotate quadrilateral Q about the centre O by 90°, clockwise.

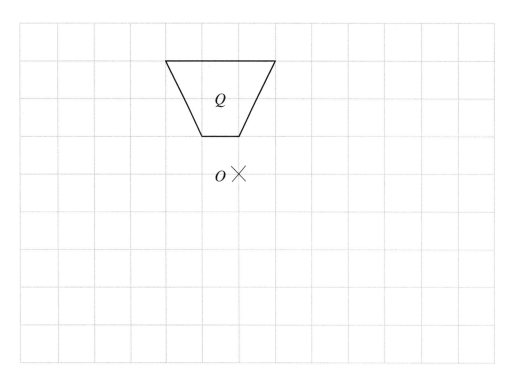

[1]

9 The table shows the sizes of 90 apples.

Size	Number of apples
Small	25
Medium	35
Large	30

Draw a pie chart to represent this information.

[3]

10 Tia and Maryam share 45 postage stamps in the ratio 2 : 7

Calculate the number of stamps that Maryam receives.

_____

[2]

11 The diagram shows two rhombuses drawn on a grid.

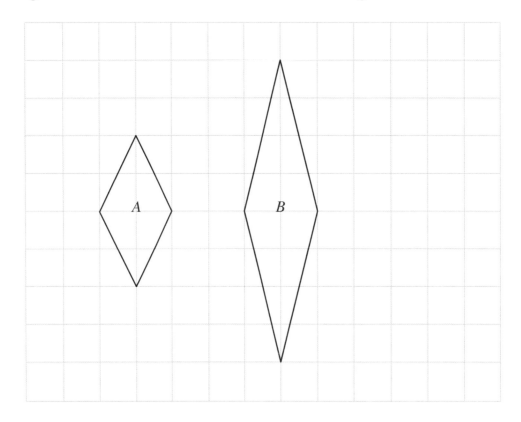

Chetan says that Rhombus B is an enlargement of Rhombus A.

Tick (✓) to show if Chetan is correct or not.

Chetan is correct ☐   Chetan is not correct ☐

Give a reason for your answer.

_____

_____

[1]

12 Here is a recipe to make biscuits.

> **Recipe**
> 70 g sugar
> 200 g flour
> 130 g butter
> 2 eggs
> 40 g dried fruit
>
> *Makes 20 biscuits*

Amir has 320 g of flour.
He has lots of the other ingredients.

Find how many of these biscuits Amir can make.

[2]

Part 2: Calculators allowed

You may use a calculator for this part of the Assessment Task.

13 Draw a ring around the ratio that is equivalent to 1 : 4

     2 : 5   0.5 : 2   4 : 14   0.4 : 1

[1]

14 A school sells 120 tickets for a concert.

Tickets are either for a child or for an adult.
The waffle diagram shows the number of each type of ticket it sells.

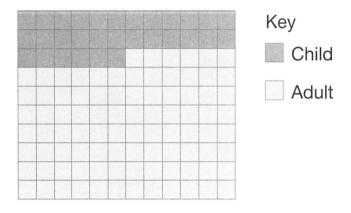

Key

▨ Child

☐ Adult

Draw a ring around the percentage of child tickets sold.

     25%   30%   75%   90%

[1]

15 Draw a ring around the number that completes this statement.

12 out of 25 = _____%

     12   30   40   48

[1]

16 A rectangle R is shown on the grid.

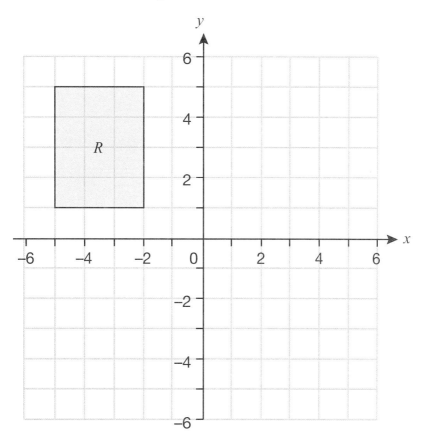

Reflect rectangle R in the y-axis.

[1]

17 (a) Find 400% of $75

$ _____

[1]

(b) Find 0.4% of 4500

_____

[1]

18 An interval is defined by the inequality $x < 9$

Draw a ring around all the values in the list below that are included in this interval.

11   8.3   0   9   12.5

[1]

19 The table shows the wheel diameter and the mass of five bicycles.

Diameter (cm)	65	70	68	60	72
Mass (kg)	14.8	19.4	17.6	16.2	17.8

Draw a scatter graph to show this information.

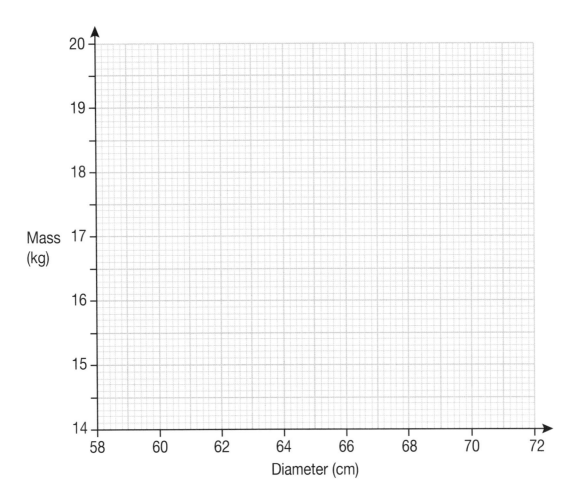

[2]

20 Write a number in each gap to make correct statements.

The distance between (3, 4) and (3, 9) is _____ units.

The distance between (6, 7) and (_____, 7) is 2 units.

The distance between (1, _____) and (4, 5) is 3 units.

[2]

21 Zoya thinks of a number, n.

She multiplies it by 6 and then she adds 4
Her answer is 52

By forming and solving an equation in n, find the number Zoya first thought of.

$n =$ _____

[2]

22 A triangle T is shown on the grid.

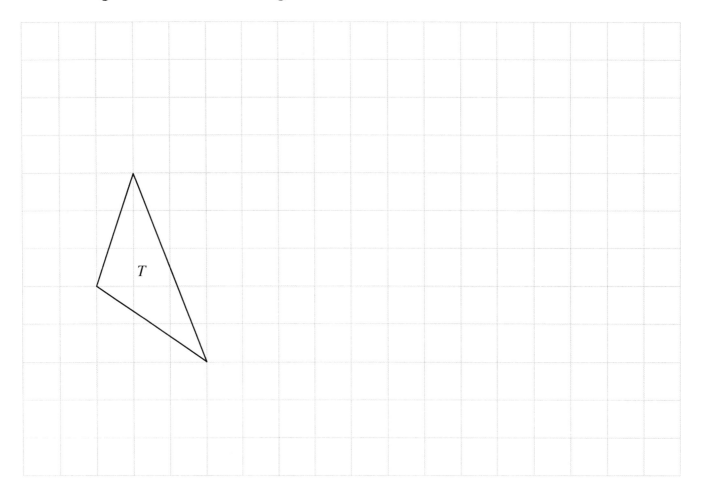

Enlarge triangle T by scale factor 2

[2]

23 Solve the equation $35 - 4y = 7$

$y =$ _____

[2]

24 A shop sells lemons and oranges.

Sophia buys 3 lemons for $0.96

Jagesh buys 7 oranges for $2.59

Yelda has $10
She buys 8 lemons.

Show that Yelda can buy at most 20 oranges with the money she has remaining.

[3]

Total marks: 40

Assessment Task 5: Self-assessment

Enter the marks for each question in the unshaded cells below.

Question	Transformations	Percentages	Presenting and interpreting data 2	Equations and inequalities	Ratio and proportion
1					
2					
3					
4					
5					
6					
7					
8					
9					
10					
11					
12					
13					
14					
15					
16					
17					
18					
19					
20					
21					
22					
23					
24					
Total	/9	/5	/8	/8	/10

Some of the questions test your skills at Thinking and Working Mathematically.
Write your marks for these questions in the grid below.

Question number	6	11	18	20	24	Total
Thinking and working mathematically						/9

The areas of the test that I am pleased with are

_____

_____

_____

The areas of the test that I found harder are

_____

_____

_____

Set yourself TWO targets.

TARGET 1

_____

_____

TARGET 2

_____

_____

Assessment Task 6

Answer **all** questions.
Total marks for this Assessment Task: 40
You will need mathematical instruments.

> Topics tested:
> Chapter 23: Probability 2
> Chapter 24: Sequences
> Chapter 25: Accurate drawing
> Chapter 26: Thinking statistically
> Chapter 27: Relationships and graphs

Part 1: Calculators not allowed

Do not use a calculator for this part of the Assessment Task.

1 A line has equation $y = x + 5$
   Draw a ring around the coordinates of a point that lies on the line.

   (0, 0)   (1, 5)   (2, 10)   (3, 8)   [1]

2 Maddie has a spinner.
   She spins it 40 times.
   The spinner lands on the blue section on 10 of the spins.

   Draw a ring around the relative frequency of the spinner landing on the
   blue section.

   0.1   0.14   0.25   0.4   [1]

3 The table shows how the students in two classes travelled to school on one day.

	Walk	Car	Bus
Class A	17	5	8
Class B	19	2	10

   Draw a ring around the most appropriate diagram for showing the information
   in the table.

   Scatter diagram   Dual bar chart

   Line graph   Venn diagram   [1]

4 The nth term of a sequence is given by the formula $n + 9$

(a) Find the 4th term in the sequence.

_____

[1]

(b) Which term in the sequence is equal to 16?

_____

[1]

5 **(a)** Draw a line parallel to the line AB that passes through point C.

[1]

(b) Draw a line perpendicular to the line PQ that passes through point R.

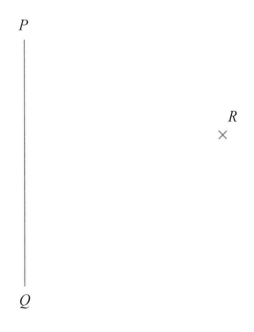

[1]

6 **(a)** y is equal to 20 more than x.

Write this rule as a linear function.

$y =$ _____

[1]

(b) 1 dollar = 80 rupees.

d = number of dollars and r = number of rupees.

Write a rule connecting r and d.

_____

[1]

7 Sienna wants to find the average colour of front doors for the houses on her street.

She says, "I will use the median."

Tick (✓) to show if the median is a suitable average for Sienna to use.

Median is appropriate ☐   Median is not appropriate ☐

Give a reason for your answer.

_____

_____

[1]

8   Karl draws this waffle diagram to show the types of fruit tree growing in a field.

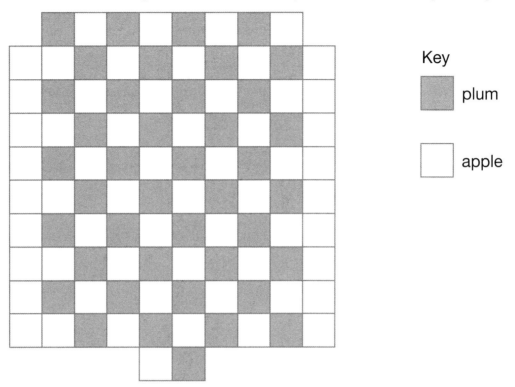

Key

plum

apple

Draw the waffle diagram in a more appropriate way so that it is easier to compare the number of each type of tree in the field.

Key

plum

apple

[3]

9 **(a)** Complete the table of values for $y = x + 4$

x	−2	−1	0	1	2	3	4
y			4				

[1]

(b) Draw the graph of $y = x + 4$ for values of x between −2 and 4

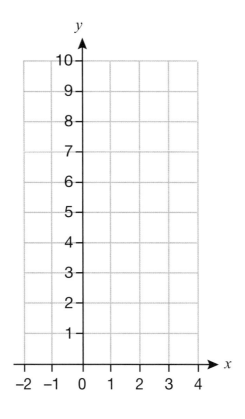

[2]

10 Complete the gaps with two numbers chosen from the box.

A biased dice is thrown _____ times.

The dice lands on 6 on _____ of the throws.

The relative frequency of getting a 6 is $\frac{3}{20}$

3	
	10
12	
	25
80	
	100

[1]

11 The diagram shows a sketch of a quadrilateral.

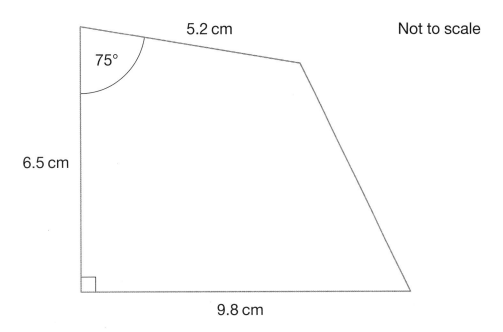

Not to scale

5.2 cm

75°

6.5 cm

9.8 cm

Use a ruler, set square and protractor to draw this quadrilateral accurately.

[3]

Part 2: Calculators allowed

You may use a calculator for this part of the Assessment Task.

12 Here is an object made from 6 cubes.

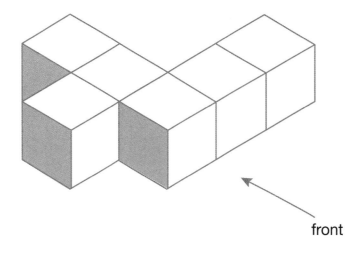

front

Draw a ring around the front elevation of the object.

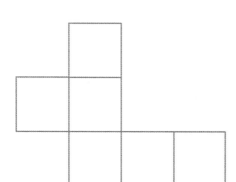

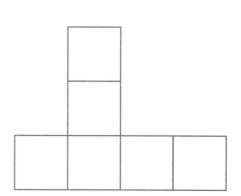

[1]

13 The term-to-term rule of a sequence is 'add 3'

The first term of the sequence is 4

Draw a ring around the 5th term in the sequence.

8   13   16   19

[1]

14 Raj draws a plan of his bedroom using a scale of 1 cm : 0.5 m
On the plan, one of his walls has a length of 8 cm.

Draw a ring around the real length of this wall.

| 4 m | 7.5 m | 8 m | 16 m | [1] |

15 Match the equation of each line to the correct description.

$x = 5$

$y = 4$

$y = -2$

Parallel to the x-axis

Parallel to the y-axis

[1]

16 Write the missing terms in this linear sequence.

31, 24, _____, 10, _____

[1]

17 Geeta and Karin each conduct an experiment by repeatedly throwing a biased coin.
Here are their results.

	Geeta's results	Karin's results
Heads	17	46
Tails	33	74

(a) Use Geeta's results to estimate the probability that the coin lands on heads.

_____

[1]

(b) Explain why Karin's results would give a better estimate of the probability than Geeta's results.

_____

_____

[1]

18 A school records the number of students absent on each of the last 10 days.

5   7   4   8   27   6   3   5   7   9

(a) Find the mean number of students absent.

_____

[2]

(b) Find the median number of students absent.

_____

[1]

(c) The school wants to use the average that best represents the data.

Tick (✓) the average they should use.

mean ☐   median ☐

Give a reason for your answer.

_____

_____

[1]

19 The first four terms of a sequence are 7, 8, 9, 10

Write down the nth term rule for the sequence.

_____

[1]

20 A map is drawn to a scale of 1 : 50 000
A lake is 1200 metres in length.

Find the length of the lake on the map.
Give your answer in centimetres.

_____ cm

[2]

21 The travel graph shows Amol's journey from his home to his friend's house.

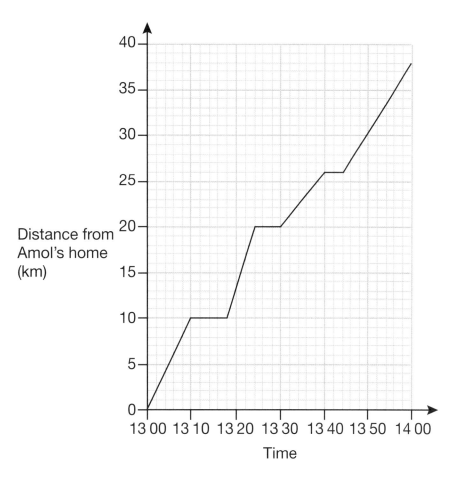

Distance from Amol's home (km)

Time

(a) Amol arrives at his friend's house at 14 00

Find the distance from Amol's house to his friend's house.

_____ km

[1]

(b) Amol stopped three times on the journey.

Find the total amount of time that Amol was not moving.

_____ minutes

[1]

22 This graph can be used to convert between US dollars and Saudi riyal.

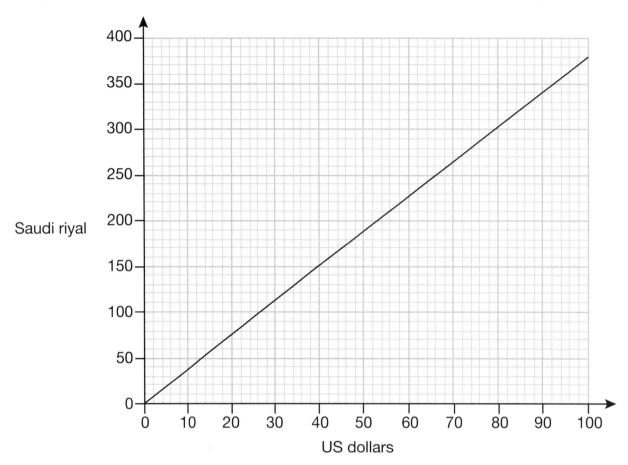

In the United States, a phone costs $800
In Saudi Arabia, the same phone costs 3100 Saudi riyal.

Use this information and the graph to find the difference in the cost of the phone in the two countries.

Give your answer in Saudi riyal.

_____ Saudi riyal

[2]

23 Finn makes a sequence of shapes from square tiles.

The diagram shows the first three shapes in his sequence.

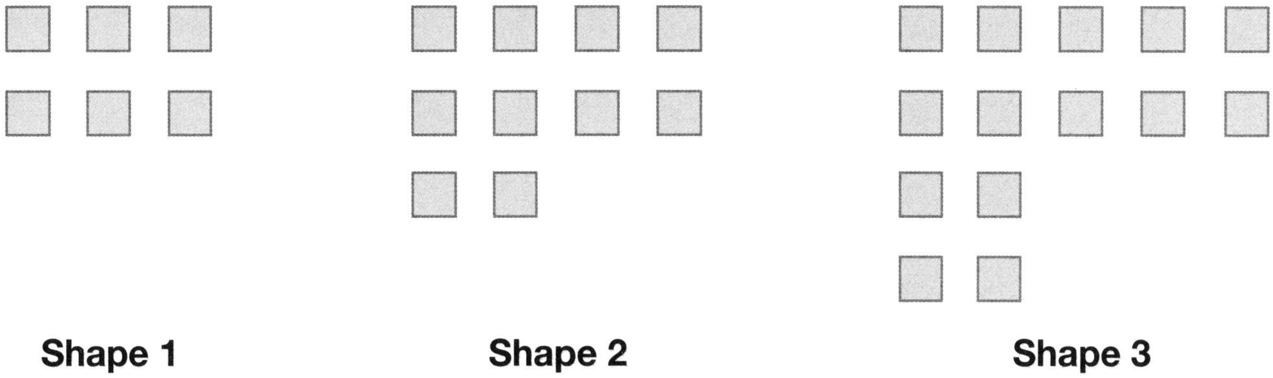

Shape 1   **Shape 2**   **Shape 3**

Find the number of square tiles needed to make Shape 8.

....

[2]

Assessment Task 6: Self-assessment

Enter the marks for each question in the unshaded cells below.

Question	Probability 2	Sequences	Accurate drawing	Thinking statistically	Relationships and graphs
1					
2					
3					
4					
5					
6					
7					
8					
9					
10					
11					
12					
13					
14					
15					
16					
17					
18					
19					
20					
21					
22					
23					
Total	/4	/7	/9	/9	/11

Some of the questions test your skills at Thinking and Working Mathematically. Write your marks for these questions in the grid below.

Question number	7	8	10	15	17(b)	18(c)	23	Total
Thinking and working mathematically								/10

The areas of the test that I am pleased with are

_____

_____

_____

The areas of the test that I found harder are

_____

_____

_____

Set yourself TWO targets.

TARGET 1

_____

_____

TARGET 2

_____

_____

End of Book Test: Paper 1

Answer **all** questions.
Total marks for this paper: 50
You will need mathematical instruments for this test.

Calculators not allowed

1   The diagram shows a circle and a line that touches it at one point.

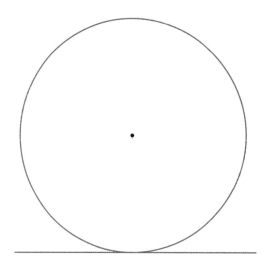

Draw a ring around the name given to this type of line.

      tangent   chord   diameter   radius

[1]

2   Draw a ring around the value of 3×10^4

      120   3000   30 000   810 000

[1]

3   Draw a ring around the expression that is equivalent to $5k - k + 2k$.

      $2k$ $4k$ $6k$ $8k$

[1]

4 A pyramid has a hexagonal base.

Draw a ring around the number of edges that the pyramid has.

　　　　6　　　　　　　　　7　　　　　　　　　8　　　　　　　　12

[1]

5 Draw a ring around the value of –2 – (–6)

　　　　4　　　　　　　　　8　　　　　　　　–8　　　　　　　　–4

[1]

6 The pie chart shows the favourite flavours of ice cream for 120 people.

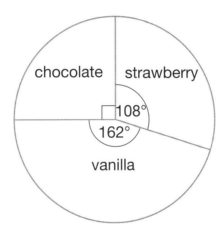

Draw a ring around the number of people who said strawberry was their favourite flavour.

　　30　　　　　　　　36　　　　　　　　54　　　　　　　　108

[1]

7 Tick (✓) to show if each statement is true or false.

	True	False
$\sqrt{36} = 6$	☐	☐
$2^3 = 6$	☐	☐
$\sqrt[3]{18} = 6$	☐	☐

[1]

8 **(a)** Here is a function machine.

Complete this mapping diagram for the function machine.

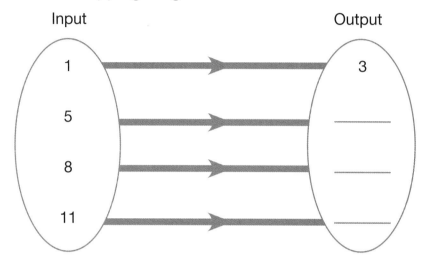

[2]

(b) Here is an input-output table for a different function machine.

Input	Output
1	5
4	20
7	35

Write the rule in the function machine.

[1]

9 Write 0.9 as a fraction and as a percentage.

Fraction _____   Percentage _____%

[1]

10 Here is a triangle T.

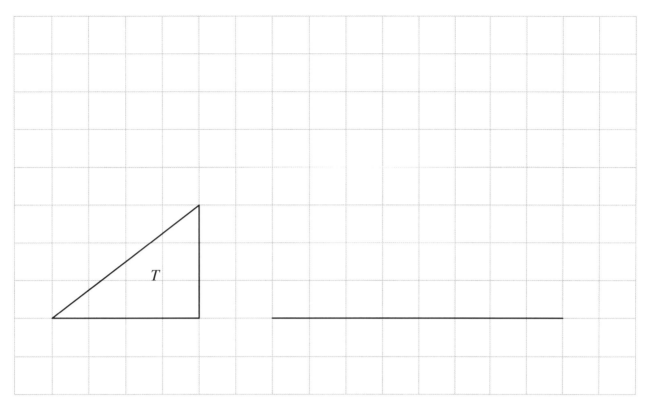

Draw on the grid an enlargement of triangle T, scale factor 2
One side has been drawn for you.

[1]

11 Iqbal counts the number of eggs in 20 bird nests.

Number of eggs	Frequency
4	7
5	5
6	6
7	2

(a) Write down the modal number of eggs in a nest.

_____

[1]

(b) Find the range of the number of eggs.

_____

[1]

12 (a) Find $\frac{1}{4} \times \frac{3}{7}$

_____

[1]

(b) Find $\frac{5}{8} \div \frac{3}{4}$

Simplify your answer.

_____

[2]

13 The diagram shows three angles around a point.

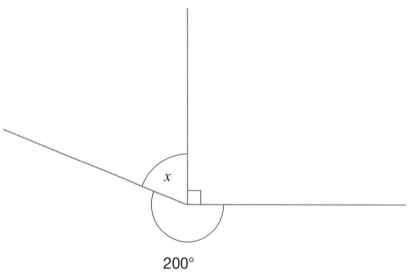

Not to scale

Find the size of the angle x.

$x =$ _____ °

[1]

14 Write each of the numbers below in the Carroll diagram to show if they are divisible by 4 or by 9.

128 774 252 436 546

	Divisible by 4	Not divisible by 4
Divisible by 9		
Not divisible by 9		

[2]

15 (a) Calculate 20 + 12 ÷ 3

_____

[1]

(b) Complete the calculation below by writing a whole number or decimal in each gap.

2.3 × 11 = 2.3 × (10 + _____) = 23 + _____ = _____

[2]

16 (a) Write down the equation of a line that is parallel to the y-axis.

_____

[1]

(b) Write down the equation of the line that passes through (2, 4) and is parallel to the x-axis.

_____

[1]

17 The diagram shows a prism made from joining two cuboids.

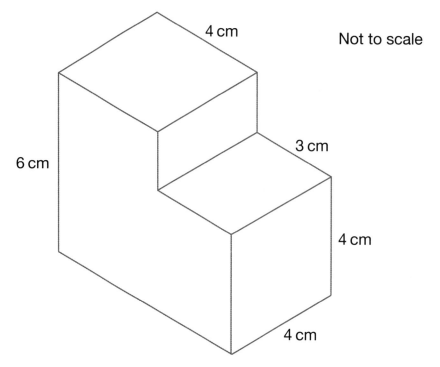

4 cm

Not to scale

3 cm

6 cm

4 cm

4 cm

Calculate the volume of the prism.

_____ cm³

[2]

18 Draw the graph of $y = x - 1$ for values of x between –2 and 3

You may use the table to help you.

x	–2	–1	0	1	2	3
y						

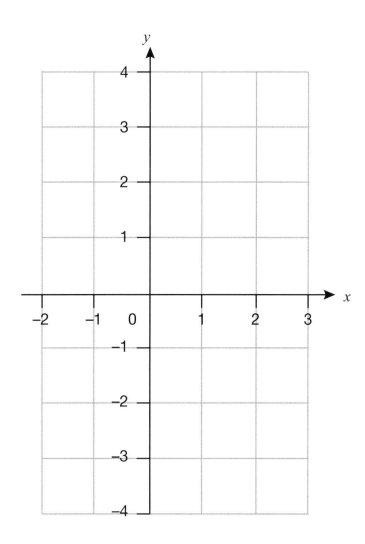

[2]

19 A bag contains 12 cards.

Each card has a regular polygon drawn on it.

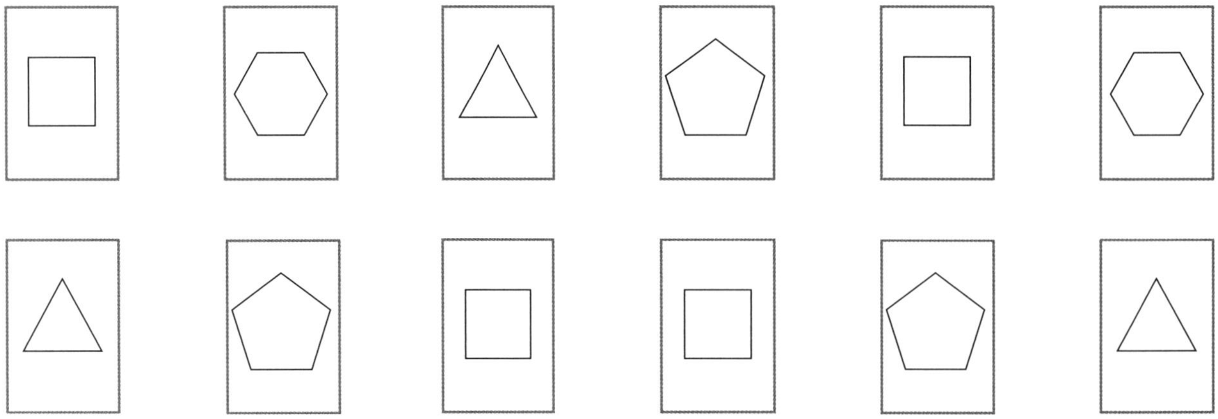

A card is picked at random from the bag.

Find the probability that the card:

(a) contains a triangle

_____

[1]

(b) has a shape with more than 4 sides.

_____

[1]

20 A cake has mass 120 grams.
Antonio cuts the cake into two pieces in the ratio 3 : 5

Find the mass of the smaller piece.

_____ grams

[2]

21 Each statement below is incorrect.

Statement 1: *The lowest common multiple of 8 and 12 is 96*

Statement 2: *The highest common factor of 36 and 48 is 6*

Write each statement to make it correct.

Statement 1: *The lowest common multiple of 8 and 12 is* _____

Statement 2: *The highest common factor of 36 and 48 is* _____

[2]

22 A pentagon P is shown on the grid.

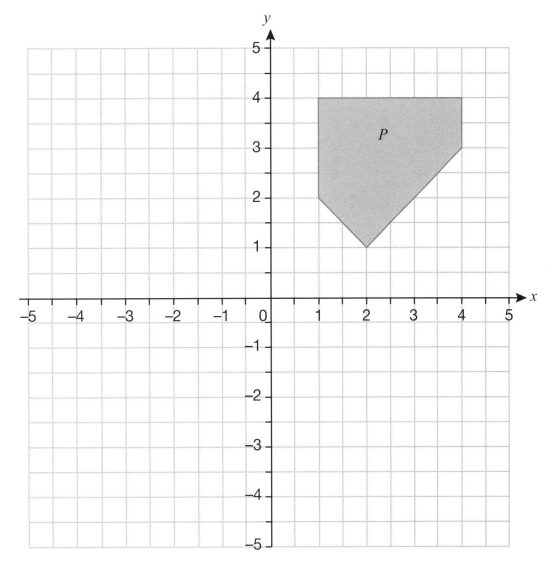

Reflect pentagon P in the y-axis.

[1]

23 Find the value of $3\frac{5}{6} + 1\frac{4}{9}$

Give your answer as a mixed number in its simplest form.

_____

[2]

24 Complete these two statements by writing integers.

(a) $6 \times (-7) =$ _____

[1]

(b) _____ ÷ _____ = −8

[1]

25 The diagram shows a kite.

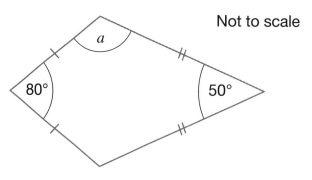

Find the size of angle a.

$a =$ _____ °

[2]

26 $3x + 2 = 38$

Find the value of $2x + 3$

_____

[3]

27 Rhianna asks some adults and some children to vote for their favourite type of fruit.

The table summarises her results.

Type of fruit	Adults	Children
Banana	10	19
Apple	8	6
Mango	22	15

Draw a compound bar chart to represent Rhianna's data.
Remember to complete the key and the axes.

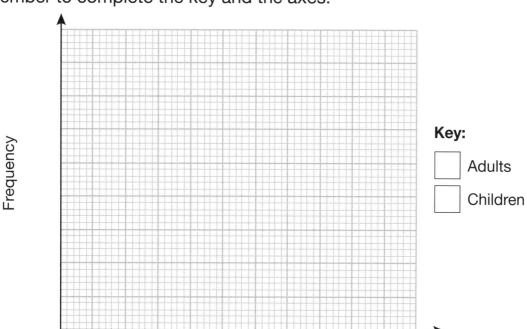

Key:

☐ Adults

☐ Children

Type of fruit

[3]

28 Work out 4.6 + 1.65 − 7.942

_____

[2]

Total marks: ____
            50

End of Book Test: Paper 2

Answer **all** questions.
Total marks for this paper: 50
You will need mathematical instruments for this test.
You may find tracing paper useful.

Calculators allowed

1 If $m = 6$, find the value of $4\,m$.

Draw a ring around the answer.

10   24   46   64

[1]

2 Draw a ring around the one statement that is true.

$0.25 < 0.2$ $0.194 > 0.6$ $0.034 < 0.12$ $0.587 > 0.6$

[1]

3 An ordinary six-sided dice is thrown.

Draw a ring around the term that describes the chance that the dice will land on a number greater than 1.

certain   unlikely   even chance   probable

[1]

4 A square has an area of $1\,cm^2$.

Not to scale

1 cm

Draw a ring around the area of the square in mm^2.

$10\,mm^2$ $100\,mm^2$ $1000\,mm^2$ $10\,000\,mm^2$

[1]

5 Draw a ring around the number of lines of symmetry in a regular octagon.

2   4   8   16

[1]

6 Water is poured into a container which is wider at the bottom than at the top.

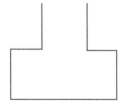

Draw a ring around the graph that shows the height of water in the container plotted against time.

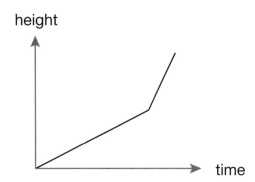

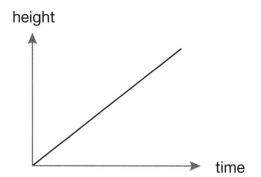

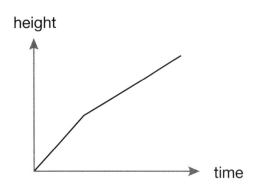

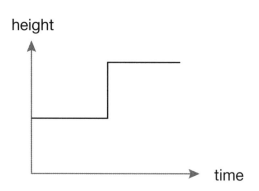

[1]

7 Here is an expression:

$$4t + 7$$

Draw lines to show if each statement is true or false.

The coefficient of t is 4

4t is a constant

7 is a term in the expression

True

False

[1]

8 A lion is n years old.

(a) An elephant is 16 years older than the lion.

Write an expression in terms of n for the age (in years) of the elephant.

_____

[1]

(b) A giraffe is four times as old as the lion.

Write an expression in terms of n for the age (in years) of the giraffe.

_____

[1]

9 Simplify the ratio 25 : 35

_____ : _____

[1]

10 A shop sells loaves of bread.

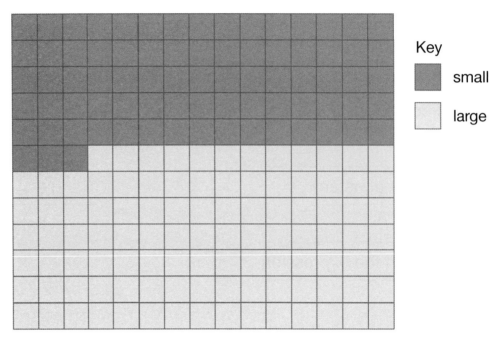

The diagram shows the number of small loaves and the number of large loaves it sold one day.

Compare the number of small loaves sold with the number of large loaves sold.

_____

_____

[1]

11 The diagram shows an angle a.

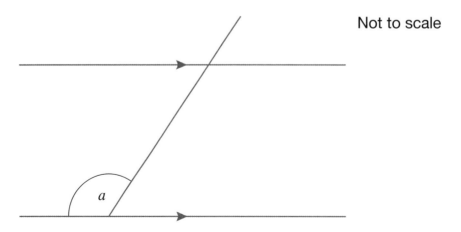

Mark on the diagram two other angles that have the same size as angle a.

[1]

12 Here is a sequence of patterns made from straight lines.

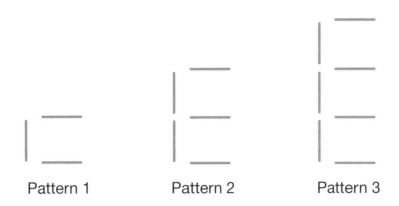

Pattern 1   Pattern 2   Pattern 3

(a) Complete the table.

Pattern number	1	2	3
Number of lines	3		

[1]

(b) Find the number of lines needed to make Pattern 5

_____

[1]

13 The diagram shows two congruent triangles.

Not to scale

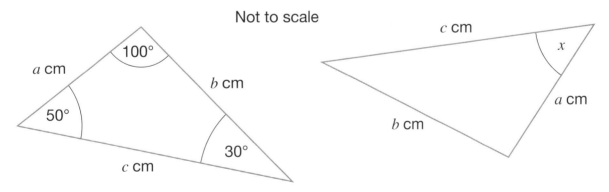

Write down the size of angle x.

$x =$ _____ °

[1]

14 Here is a fair spinner with coloured sections.

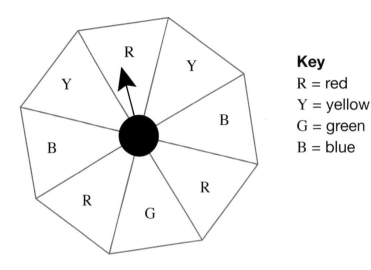

Key
R = red
Y = yellow
G = green
B = blue

The spinner is spun.

Tick (✓) to show if these statements are true or false.

	True	False
The possible outcomes are red, yellow, green and blue	☐	☐
The probability the spinner lands on red is $\frac{1}{4}$	☐	☐

[1]

15 The diagram shows an open interval.

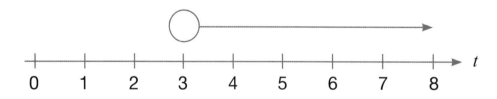

Write this interval as an inequality.

t _____

[1]

16 (a) Complete the descriptions of the symmetrical properties of each shape.

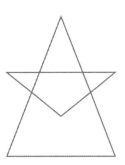

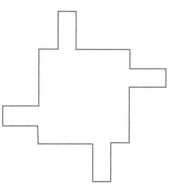

Number of lines of symmetry = _____
Rotational symmetry of order _____

Number of lines of symmetry = _____
Rotational symmetry of order _____

[2]

(b) Here is a square divided into triangles and smaller squares.

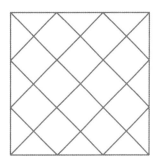

Shade 2 triangles and 4 squares to make a pattern with:

- 2 lines of symmetry **and**
- rotational symmetry of order 2

[1]

17 (a) Round 0.284 to 2 decimal places.

_____

[1]

(b) Round 0.47965 to 3 decimal places.

_____

[1]

18 The coordinates of four points are as follows.

$A(4, 2)$ $B(4, 8)$ $C(10, 8)$ $D(4, 10)$

(a) Find the distance between A and D.

_____ units

[1]

(b) Complete each statement using one of the symbols <, > or =

Distance between A and B _____ Distance between B and C

Distance between A and B _____ Distance between B and D

[1]

19 A quadrilateral is shown on the grid.

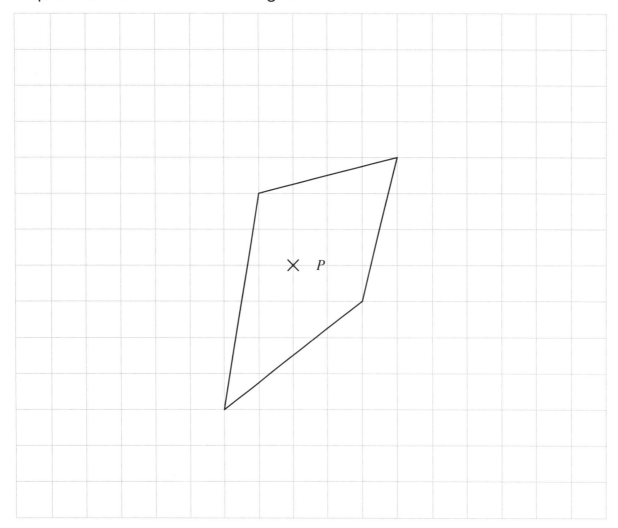

Rotate the quadrilateral by 90° clockwise, centre point P.

[2]

20 Lucy designs a questionnaire to find out the number of times people visited a gym last month.

Here is her question.

> How many times did you visit the gym last month?
> Tick (✓) your answer.
>
> 0–2 ☐   2–4 ☐   4–6 ☐

Write down one problem with her answer options.

_____

_____

[1]

21 (a) Expand $9(4w - 3)$

_____

[1]

(b) Simplify.
$$\frac{11y}{12} - \frac{4y}{12}$$

_____

[1]

22 (a) Find 105% of $480

$_____

[1]

(b) Anneka has 60 books.

12 of her books are history books.

Find the percentage of her books that are history books.

_____%

[2]

23 The diagram shows a sketch of a 3D object.

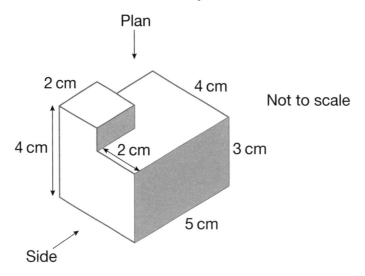

Plan

2 cm   4 cm

Not to scale

4 cm   2 cm   3 cm

5 cm

Side

(a) Tina draws this incorrect plan view of the object on squared paper.

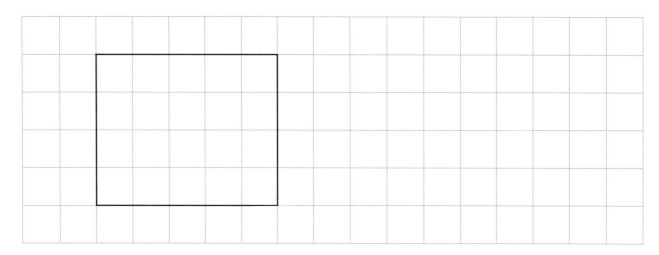

Change Tina's plan view so that it is correct.

[1]

(b) Draw a side elevation of the object from the direction shown on the diagram.

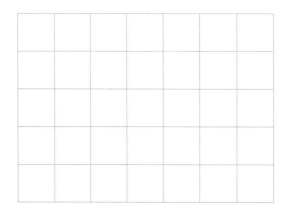

[1]

24 The table shows the ages of some coins.

Age of coin (years)	Frequency
0–5	17
5–10	28
10–15	16
15–20	10
20–25	4

Draw a frequency diagram to show this information.

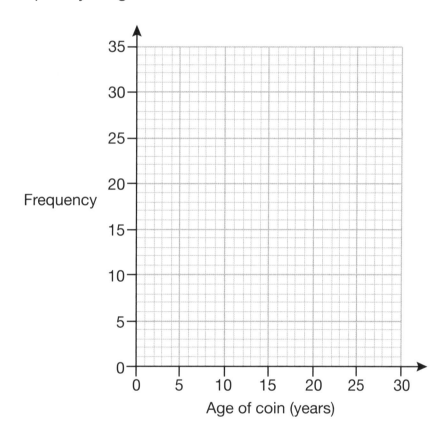

[2]

25 Calculate the area of this shape.

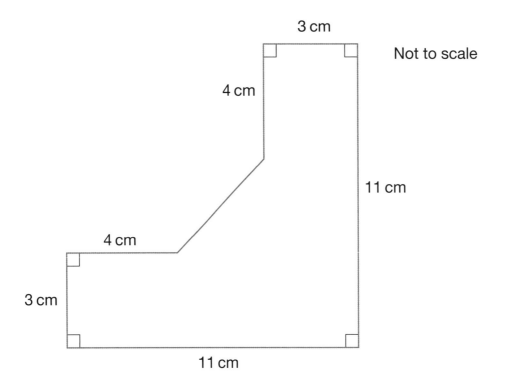

3 cm

Not to scale

4 cm

11 cm

4 cm

3 cm

11 cm

_____ cm²

[2]

26 (a) Krishnan tosses a biased coin repeatedly.

Here are his results.

Outcome	Frequency
Heads	44
Tails	36

Use Krishnan's results to find the relative frequency of his coin landing on a head.

Give your answer as a decimal.

_____

[2]

(b) Georgia throws the same coin **more times** than Krishnan.
She gets the same relative frequency of throwing a head as Krishnan.

Complete the table to show possible results for Georgia.

Outcome	Frequency
Heads	
Tails	

[1]

27 400 South African rand = 3100 Japanese yen.
Kofi buys a television for 27 125 Japanese yen.

Work out the cost of the television in South African rand.

_____ South African rand

[2]

28 Here is a sketch of a trapezium.

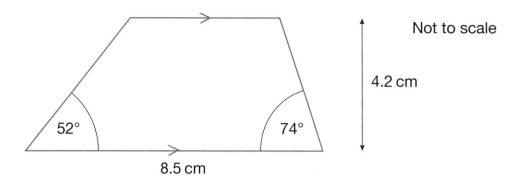

Use mathematical instruments to draw the trapezium accurately.

[2]

29 The first term of Anton's sequence is 41
The term-to-term rule of his sequence is 'subtract 4'

Suzie has a different sequence.
The nth term of Suzie's sequence is $3n$

Write a number to complete the following statement.

The 6th term in Anton's sequence is equal to the _____*th term in Suzie's sequence.*

[2]

30 The points (–4, 1), (0, 4) and (1, 12) are all transformed by the same translation.

(–4, 1) is mapped to the point $(a, -4)$

(0, 4) is mapped to the point $(6, b)$

(1, 12) is mapped to the point (c, c)

Show that $a + b + c$ is a multiple of 4

[3]

Total marks: ———
50

End of Book Test: Self-assessment

Enter the mark for each question for Paper 1 and Paper 2 in the unshaded cells.

Paper 1

Question	Number	Algebra	Geometry and Measure	Statistics and Probability
1				
2				
3				
4				
5				
6				
7				
8				
9				
10				
11				
12				
13				
14				
15				
16				
17				
18				
19				
20				
21				
22				
23				
24				
25				
26				
27				
28				
Total P1	/22	/11	/9	/8

Paper 2

Question	Number	Algebra	Geometry and Measure	Statistics and Probability
1				
2				
3				
4				
5				
6				
7				
8				
9				
10				
11				
12				
13				
14				
15				
16				
17				
18				
19				
20				
21				
22				
23				
24				
25				
26				
27				
28				
29				
30				
Total P2	/9	/12	/20	/9

Overall total Paper 1 + Paper 2:

Total	/31	/23	/29	/17

Total mark: _____ /100

Thinking and working mathematically

Some of the questions test your skills at Thinking and Working Mathematically.
Write your marks for these questions in the grids below.

Paper 1

Question number	7	8(b)	14	16(a)	16(b)	21	24(b)	Total
Thinking and working mathematically								/9

Paper 2

Question number	7	12(b)	14	16(b)	20	23(a)	26(b)	30	Total
Thinking and working mathematically									/10

Overall total: _____ /19

The areas of the test that I am pleased with are

_____

_____

_____

The areas of the test that I found harder are

_____

_____

_____

Set yourself THREE targets.

TARGET 1

_____

_____

TARGET 2

_____

_____

TARGET 3

_____

_____